FROM FELON

Gun rights restored

TO FREEDOM

A Step-by-Step guide
Gun restoration in
Ohio

Apply under your state law

FROM FELON TO FREEDOM
GUN RIGHTS RESTORED

A STEP-BY-STEP GUIDE TO GUN RESTORATION IN OHIO

DISCLAIMER: THIS BOOK IS FOR INFORMATIONAL AND EDUCATIONAL PURPOSES ONLY AND DOES NOT CONSTITUTE LEGAL ADVICE. LAWS AND POLICIES CAN CHANGE, AND OUTCOMES VARY BY INDIVIDUAL CIRCUMSTANCES. FOR LEGAL ADVICE ABOUT YOUR SPECIFIC SITUATION, CONSULT A LICENSED ATTORNEY IN YOUR JURISDICTION.

PUBLISHER: BLINKS GO BANG PUBLISHING
WEBSITE: MY-RIGHTSRESTORED.COM
EMAIL: BLINXGOBANG@GMAIL
FIRST EDITION: 2025
PRINTED IN THE UNITED STATES OF AMERICA

INTRODUCTION

"HELPING ONE PERSON MIGHT NOT CHANGE THE WHOLE WORLD, BUT IT COULD CHANGE THE WORLD FOR ONE PERSON."

I was born in 1973, raised in the 80's, where the crack era had exploded, and also raised in the 90's where the influence of Chicago and Los Angeles gang banging had spread to almost every community through out the United States, (N.W.A era) By the time I was 13 years old in middle school, 8th grade to be exact, I had shot a high school kid who was with a group of other high school kids that would repeatedly rob me and my friends of our belongings on our long walk home from school.

By the time I was 14, I was arrested as a juvenile for carrying a concealed weapon, a .25 caliber pistol. By the time I was 17, I graduated, not from high school but to a one-way trip to prison for armed robbery of a gas station

If you're reading this book, you've probably entered a point of your life where you're trying to change or have already changed your lifestyle

I don't care where you come from, I don't care what you've done, the only thing I care about is providing motivation for that change and to help you move forward in the process of getting your gun rights back.

INTRODUCTION

Since you've spent your hard earned money on this ebook, you probably already have the motivation, so I'll provide you with my gun restoration journey for an example of things you may encounter along the way, and a Step-by-Step guide of what you'll need to apply.

Life is very difficult to push through some days, but getting goals accomplished is very satisfying and builds confidence. At the time of my writing this ebook, my mother passed away from cancer, and my motivation is still as high as ever to complete this goal

I've put my heart and soul into this book. I've left no stone unturned, no area uncovered. As I recollect what I did to restore my gun rights and gather the necessary information, you'll need to move forward in this easy to understand ebook, ...LET'S GOOO!!!..

Be on the lookout for my book

"From Felon to 6 Figures"

INTRODUCTION LINKS

CHECK OUT THESE 3 VIDEO LINKS

Check out these 3 videos on YouTube, to hear actual courtroom stories. You can learn about new federal laws, and watch a felon make an actual gun purchase.

Now, Let's Go For Real!!!!

Blinxgobang@gmail.com

BLINXGOBANG

CONTENTS

CONTENTS

1

CHAPTER

STATE VS FEDERAL LAW

BRIEF SUMMARY OF STATE VS FEDERAL LAWS

Restoring your state conviction gun rights is very confusing trying to understand if you qualify between state and federal laws, each with its own processes and requirements. While some states offer pathways to restore firearm rights in state court, these may not align with federal regulations. For instance, certain states may restore gun rights at the state level, but without federal recognition, (My state, the state of Ohio is recognized after a state restoration in state court by federal law). My paperwork was sent to my local sheriffs office, I was cleared for my CCW license and have purchased several weapons passing the Federal NICS background check, other states may still face restrictions under federal law, check your state. Additionally, federal ways for restoring gun rights, such as through the Bureau of Alcohol, Tobacco, Firearms and Explosives (ATF), have been defunded since 1992, good news for federally convicted felons the (DOJ) Department of Justice has taken over the fed restoration process from the ATF as of 2/6/2025 *SEE* www.federalregister.com for more info, also look into 18 U.S.C925c. This brief summary is to give you a quick glimpse into Understanding the interplay between state and federal laws, you must check your state, I can only give you my journey and the facts that I encountered, This is not legal advise, seek legal representation if needed.

CHAPTER 2

Explaining O.R.C 2923.14

Explaining

O.R.C 2923.14

Read it, Read it, Read it, and READ IT AGAIN!

My first step in restoring my gun rights was googling Relief from weapons disabilities and I found the (ORC) Ohio Revise Code 2923.14 (*SEE* https://codes.ohio.gov) this will be different in your state, for example Michigan is MCL 28.424 I'm sure you get the point I'm trying to make.

Here you'll find all the stipulations on applying, how to apply, where to apply, who's eligible, who's not eligible, for example I get this question a lot and this actually happened to me. (Do I file where I live, or where I caught my case) I caught my case in Detroit, years later I moved to Ohio and decided to try and restore my rights, figured I'd have to go back to Michigan, nope! outlined in ORC 2923.14 states file in the county in which you reside. Check YOUR state law.

OHIO LAWS
LEGISLATIVE SERVICE COMMISSION

(A)(1) Except as otherwise provided in division (A)(2) of this section, any person who is prohibited from acquiring, having, carrying, or using firearms may apply to the court of common pleas in the county in which the person resides for relief from such prohibition.

3
CHAPTER

ELIGIBILITY
O.R.C 2923.14

ELIGIBILITY

O.R.C 2923.14

WHO'S ELIGIBLE

Let's start with the mandatory three requirements

<u>1) Free from incarceration, not on parole, probation , and all fines paid</u>

since release has led a law abiding life and appears likely to continue

applicant is not otherwise prohibited from owning a firearm (fed law)

1. Applicants must be fully discharged from prison, including any parole, community control sanctions "probation", post-release control "halfway house". All court cost and fees must be paid in full. Applicant should not be under an active indictment or have any pending municipal charges. Alternatively, if the disability is based on a factor other than a conviction—such as mental health issues or drug dependency—that factor must no longer apply to the applicant. So what they're saying is if you're documented with a mental disability from a doctor, this must be cleared up first, same for a drug addiction. This requirement ensures that individuals seeking restoration have addressed the circumstances that led to their disqualification. (codes.ohio.gov)

ELIGIBILITY

O.R.C 2923.14

WHO'S ELIGIBLE

Let's start with the mandatory three requirements

Free from incarceration, not on parole or probation all fines paid

2) Since release has led a law abiding life and appears likely to continue

Applicate is not otherwise prohibited from owning a firearm(Fed law)

2. Demonstration of Law-Abiding Behavior
Applicants must show that they have led a law-abiding life since the completion of their sentence. This is demonstrated by having a good track record since release, with no negative interactions with law enforcement, no new charges, and no pending charges. You should also be working and being a productive citizen. The court assesses whether the applicant appears likely to continue this behavior in the future. I have heard of people getting their rights restored only a few years after release, all the way up to 30 years or more. Obviously, the longer you display good behavior on the streets, the better your chances, but if you only have a handful of years, it's still very possible.

ELIGIBILITY

O.R.C 2923.14

WHO'S ELIGIBLE

Let's start with the mandatory three requirements

Free from incarceration, not on parole or probation all fines paid

Since release has led a lay abiding life and appears likely to continue

3) Applicate is not otherwise prohibited from owning a firearm (Fed law)

3. Absence of Other Legal Prohibitions
Applicants must not be otherwise prohibited by law from acquiring, having, or using firearms. This includes ensuring that there are no existing federal or state legal restrictions that would disqualify the individual from possessing firearms. For 1 example in my specific case I thought I was good since I meet the above 2 requirements with ease, I didn't even understand what otherwise prohibited meant, well, I served more than 12 months in prison and federally, sentenced to or serving more than 12 months would restrict me under federal law "18 U.S.C. 922(g)" "Otherwise Prohibited" in the state of Ohio if the judge still restores your "Civil" gun rights, federally it's recognized and that's how I got restored, my packet of information gathered and my track record is what he based it on, check U.S.C 922(g) vs your states laws and identify any prohibition *SEE* next page for judges letter on this.

The judge says here that the state of Ohio "Prosecutor" objects to my restoration because I don't comply with the Federal law as you can see, he overruled that, check your laws and understand ultimately it's the judges decision.

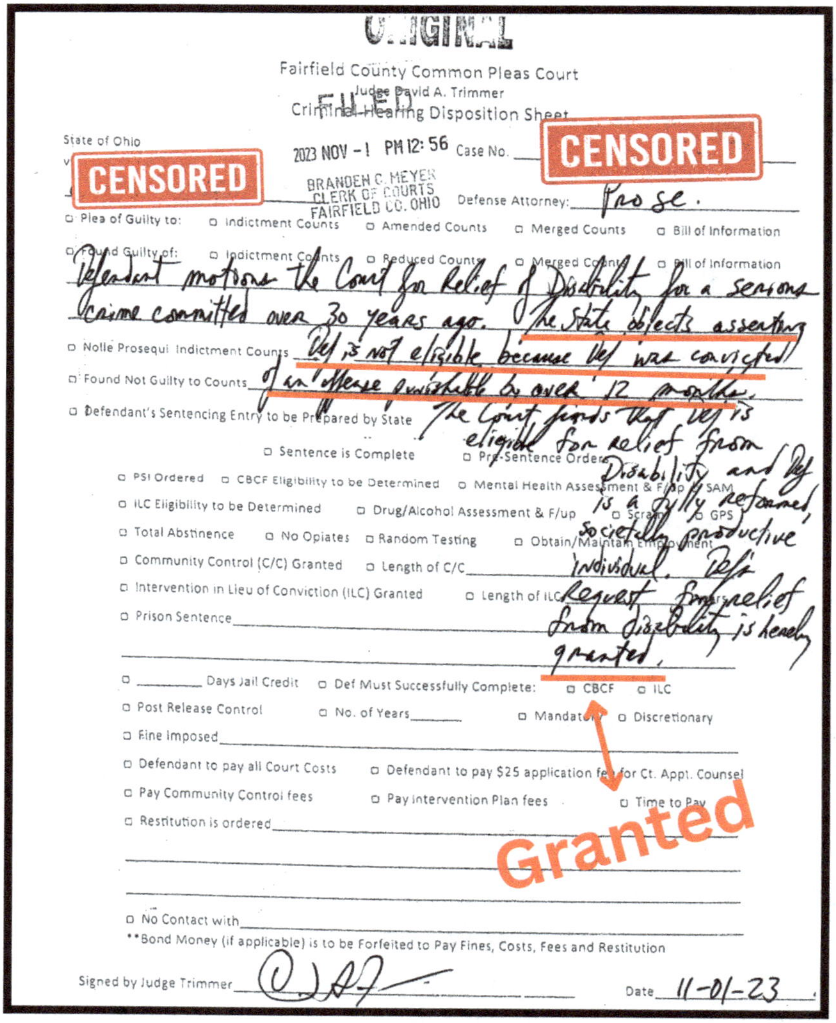

ORIGINAL

Fairfield County Common Pleas Court
Judge David A. Trimmer
Criminal Hearing Disposition Sheet

FILED
2023 NOV -1 PM 12:56
BRANDEN C. MEYER
CLERK OF COURTS
FAIRFIELD CO. OHIO

State of Ohio
v. CENSORED

Case No. CENSORED

Defense Attorney: Pro se.

☐ Plea of Guilty to: ☐ Indictment Counts ☐ Amended Counts ☐ Merged Counts ☐ Bill of Information

☐ Found Guilty of: ☐ Indictment Counts ☐ Reduced Counts ☐ Merged Counts ☐ Bill of Information

Defendant motions the Court for Relief of Disability for a serious crime committed over 30 years ago. The State objects asserting

☐ Nolle Prosequi Indictment Counts Def is not eligible because Def was convicted

☐ Found Not Guilty to Counts of an offense punishable by over 12 months.

☐ Defendant's Sentencing Entry to be Prepared by State The Court finds that Def is eligible for relief from

☐ Sentence is Complete ☐ Pre-Sentence Ordered

☐ PSI Ordered ☐ CBCF Eligibility to be Determined ☐ Mental Health Assessment & F/up ☐ SAM

☐ ILC Eligibility to be Determined ☐ Drug/Alcohol Assessment & F/up ☐ Scram ☐ GPS

☐ Total Abstinence ☐ No Opiates ☐ Random Testing ☐ Obtain/Maintain Employment

☐ Community Control (C/C) Granted ☐ Length of C/C

☐ Intervention in Lieu of Conviction (ILC) Granted ☐ Length of ILC

☐ Prison Sentence

Disability and Def is a fully reformed, societally productive individual. Def's Request for relief from disability is hereby granted.

☐ ______ Days Jail Credit ☐ Def Must Successfully Complete: ☐ CBCF ☐ ILC

☐ Post Release Control ☐ No. of Years______ ☐ Mandatory ☐ Discretionary

☐ Fine Imposed

☐ Defendant to pay all Court Costs ☐ Defendant to pay $25 application fee for Ct. Appt. Counsel

☐ Pay Community Control fees ☐ Pay Intervention Plan fees ☐ Time to Pay

☐ Restitution is ordered

Granted

☐ No Contact with

**Bond Money (if applicable) is to be Forfeited to Pay Fines, Costs, Fees and Restitution

Signed by Judge Trimmer ____________ Date 11-01-23

ELIGIBILITY

O.R.C 2923.14

Who's Not Eligible

I'll identify people not eligible in this section. If you see a category that pertains to you, go to O.R.C 2923.132. Read it and get a complete understanding of how you're not eligible, I have also included the federal disqualifying factors outlined in 18 U.S.C 922(g) some of these disqualifying factors are rectifiable, example, if you're diagnosed mentally insane because of a break down you had years ago, go get reevaluated and show proof the mental health issue is behind you. If you have other disqualifying offenses try the expungement process, state pardon by your Governor (mine is in motion) you get the point, search all avenues.

O.R.C 2923.14

Who's Not Eligible

Violent Career Criminal

A person is classified as a "Violent Career Criminal" if they have been convicted of, or pleaded guilty to, two or more "Violent Felony Offenses" (listed below) within the time frame of 8 years. Read ORC 2923.14 to understand the full outline; if not in Ohio, check your state law.

Definition of "Violent Felony Offense"

According to ORC 2923.132(A)(2), the following offenses are designated as violent felony offenses:

1. Aggravated Murder – ORC § 2903.01
2. Murder – ORC § 2903.02
3. Voluntary Manslaughter – ORC § 2903.03
4. Involuntary Manslaughter – ORC § 2903.04
5. Felonious Assault – ORC § 2903.11
6. Aggravated Assault – ORC § 2903.12
7. Kidnapping – ORC § 2905.01
8. Abduction – ORC § 2905.02
9. Aggravated Arson – ORC § 2909.02
10. Terrorism – ORC § 2909.24

ELIGIBILITY

O.R.C 2923.14

Who's Not Eligible

Definition of "Violent Felony Offense"

1. **Aggravated Robbery – ORC § 2911.01**
2. **Robbery – ORC § 2911.02**
3. **Aggravated Burglary – ORC § 2911.11**
4. **Burglary – ORC § 2911.12(A)(1) or (2)**
5. **Rape – ORC § 2907.02 (felony)**
6. **Sexual Battery – ORC § 2907.03 (felony)**
7. **Unlawful Sexual Conduct with a Minor – ORC § 2907.04 (felony)**
8. **Gross Sexual Imposition – ORC § 2907.05 (felony)**
9. **Domestic Violence – ORC § 2919.25 (felony of the third degree)**
10. **Substantially Equivalent Offenses – Felony violations of existing or former laws of Ohio, other states, or the United States that are substantially equivalent to the offenses listed above.**
11. **Conspiracy, Attempt, or Complicity – Engaging in a conspiracy or attempt to commit, or complicity in committing, any of the offenses listed above, if the conspiracy, attempt, or complicity is a felony of the first or second degree.(codes.ohio.gov, law.cornell.edu)**

ELIGIBILITY

O.R.C 2923.14

Who's Not Eligible

Here are additional O.R.C codes that are **not classified under career criminal** that you need to be aware of.

- **ORC 2941.141**
- **ORC 2941.144**
- **ORC 2941.145**
- **ORC 2941.146**
- **ORC 2941.1412**
- **ORC 2941.1424**

FEDERALLY

Who's Not Eligible

18 U.S.C 922 G

Under federal law, specifically 18 U.S.C. § 922(g), the following convictions
and circumstances disqualify a person from owning or possessing firearms.

Here they are, one by one:

● Federal Disqualifiers for Gun Ownership (18 U.S.C. § 922(g))

Felony Conviction
Anyone convicted of a crime punishable by more than one year in prison (felony under federal law), even if the sentence was less. (THE JUDGE STILL RESTORED ME)

Fugitive from Justice
A person who has fled any state to avoid prosecution or testify in a criminal case.

Unlawful User or Addicted to a Controlled Substance
Includes illegal drug users, addicts, or even legal marijuana users (despite state laws).
Medical or recreational marijuana users are disqualified, since marijuana is still illegal federally.

Mental Health Adjudication
A person adjudicated as mentally defective or committed to a mental institution.
Includes those found not guilty by reason of insanity or found incompetent to stand trial.

FEDERALLY

Who's Not Eligible

18 U.S.C 922 G

Illegal or Unlawful Alien
Anyone illegally in the U.S., or those admitted under a nonimmigrant visa (exceptions apply, like hunting license exemptions).

Dishonorable Discharge from the Armed Forces
A dishonorable military discharge bars you from owning firearms.

Renounced U.S. Citizenship
People who have formally renounced their citizenship cannot legally possess firearms.

Subject to a Domestic Violence Protection Order
Must be a court-issued order restraining the person from harassing, stalking, or threatening an intimate partner or child.
Must include a finding that the person is a credible threat or explicitly prohibits firearms.

Convicted of a Misdemeanor Crime of Domestic Violence
Includes physical force or threatened use of a deadly weapon against a spouse, cohabitant, parent, or guardian.
Even if it was a misdemeanor, it disqualifies you under federal law.
indictment (Pending Charge)
You cannot purchase a firearm if you are currently under indictment for a felony or disqualifying misdemeanor.
However, possession is still allowed unless convicted.

4

CHAPTER

THE "PACKET"

THE PACKET

In this section we'll discuss what I refer to as "The Packet" otherwise known as information you'll need on your application and documentation you'll need to go along with your application. The goal here is to include all positive things going on in your life leaving the judge no doubt that you're leading a law abiding life and appear likely to continue. I'll list the things that worked for me. I'll also list the letter that I wrote to the judge explaining why I felt I deserved my civil gun rights back. Keep in mind these things will vary person to person and are not mandatory, only application info is mandatory.

- Proof of employment letter
- Work training, promotions or awards
- Proof of business, LLC or Certificate, if any
- Accolades, schooling, community service, church, etc
- Letter to the judge
- Application with all necessary information

THE PACKET

WORK TRAINING, PROMOTIONS OR AWARDS

GE Aviation

Quality Technology Center - Nondestructive Testing

CENSORED

Has Received Practical Training in the Eddy Current Inspection of the

CF34 FAN BLADE PIN HOLES

in accordance with

EM 72-00-00, SPECIAL PROCEDURE 60

7-13-2010
Date

Jon Dierdorf

Certificate of Achievement

This is to certify that

CENSORED

has successfully completed the

FAA Safety Team Aviation Learning Center Online Course

A Case For Non Technical Training (Amt Core Course For 2021)

Course Number ALC-666 (Qualifies for 1 Hour IA Refresher Training)

Presented by FAA Safety Team 2021 AMT Core Course

June 23, 2021

Federal Aviation Administration

Certificate Number 0743136-20210623-00666

Valerie G. Palazzolo, National Manager, FAA Safety Team

THE PACKET

WORK TRAINING, PROMOTIONS OR AWARDS

U.S. Department of Transportation
Federal Aviation Administration

2019

Certificate of Training
"Silver Award"
presented to

CENSORED

For Participating in the FAA Aviation Maintenance Technician Awards Program.

Representative of the Administrator — 1/12/2020 *Date*

U.S. DEPARTMENT OF TRANSPORTATION

FEDERAL AVIATION ADMINISTRATION

AVIATION MAINTENANCE SYMPOSIUM
Certificate of Completion

CENSORED

HAS SATISFACTORILY COMPLETED ___ HOURS OF INSTRUCTION
IN
AVIATION SAFETY AND MAINTENANCE STANDARDS

Suspected Unapproved Parts Industry Training

Computer Based Training | Reproduction of this certificate is UNAUTHORIZED | 10/16/2020

THE PACKET

PROOF OF LLC'S OR BUSINESS CERTS, *IF ANY*

STATE OF OHIO
CERTIFICATE
Ohio Secretary of State, Jon Husted
4179150

It is hereby certified that the Se CENSORED ustody of the business records for

and, that said business records show the filing and recording of:

Document(s) CENSORED
DOMESTIC FOR PROFIT LLC - ARTICLES OF ORG
Effective Date: 05/10/2018

United States of America
State of Ohio
Office of the Secretary of State

Witness my hand and the seal of the Secretary of State at Columbus, Ohio this 11th day of May, A.D. 2018.

Jon Husted
Ohio Secretary of State

STATE OF OHIO
CERTIFICATE
Ohio Secretary of State, Frank LaRose
4637997

It is hereby certified that the CENSORED stody of the business records for

and, that said business records show the filing and recording of:

Document(s) CENSORED
DOMESTIC FOR PROFIT LLC - ARTICLES OF ORG
Effective Date: 03/14/2021

United States of America
State of Ohio
Office of the Secretary of State

Witness my hand and the seal of the Secretary of State at Columbus, Ohio this 18th day of March, A.D. 2021.

Frank LaRose
Ohio Secretary of State

THE PACKET

LETTER TO THE JUDGE

To whom it may concern,

Thirty two years ago, in March of 1991, at the age of seventeen, I made the worst decision of my life. I committed a crime while still in high school that landed me in prison and labeled me a felon.

Ever since the first day that I was released from prison, I was determined to change my life and prove all doubters wrong. First I removed myself from the environment in Detroit, and most importantly, I changed my circle of friends.

Fast forward, thirty two years later, I am forty nine years old. Since being released I have obtained my G.E.D, I have attended The Michigan Institute of Aeronautics, where I received my license to become an Aircraft Mechanic. I was not only hired for a job in my career field, I excelled past my peers. I have received numerous certificates and awards also, I've been promoted to Aircraft Inspector, the position that I currently hold. I am twenty six years in this field, and seventeen plus years at my current employer, Republic Airways at John Glenn International Airport. I service Delta, United, and American Airlines Aircrafts. So, if you fly, chances are I've worked on yours too.

I am currently married, I have seven children, two college graduates, two currently in college, and three grandchildren.

I have not had any return visits to prison, no convictions, nor have I had any trouble with law enforcement. I hope that the court can judge me on the last thirty two years of my life, not the beginning of it and fully understand I am a law abiding citizen, even though I am labeled a felon. I am not a criminal, I just made one bad decision.

Thank you for your consideration,

Respectfully,

CENSORED

CENSORED

THE PACKET

APPLICATION

When I went to the county clerks office to get an application to move forward in filing my petition, I was told they didn't have an application for that. I would need a lawyer to draw me up one. I don't know if that's every state or just Ohio, but no way was I spending $2,500 on a lawyer. I googled a generic version for FREE 99, they also had a paid version for a small fee. You can play with Google and look for a gun restoration application. You should be able to find a blank one that you can insert all your information in and print out. here's all the MANDATORY info you'll need.

- **Title: Your court, your county**
- **Header: Application For Relief Weapons Under Disability Pursuant to O.R.C 2923.14 or your state code**
- **Name, Address, date of birth**
- **State and county of offense, Date of offense**
- **Case # and charge(s)**
- **Sentence info , (i.e) prison, prob - start date and release date**

THE PACKET

APPLICATION

ORIGINAL

FILED

2023 AUG 11 AM 10: 41

BRANDEN C. MEYER
CLERK OF COURTS
FAIRFIELD CO. OHIO

IN THE COURT OF COMMON PLEAS
FAIRFIELD COUNTY, OHIO

IN RE:

[redacted] N
DOB: [redacted]

Name
address
D.O.B

Applicant/Petitioner

CASE NO: [redacted]

JUDGE : JUDGE [redacted]

APPLICATION FOR RELIEF
WEAPONS UNDER
DISABILITY PURSUANT
TO R.C. 2923.14

(ORAL HEARING REQUESTED)

Now comes Petitioner/Applicant, [redacted], proceeding pro se, respectfully submits this application requesting that this Court relieve the Petitioner/Applicant from his current disability prohibiting him from

APPLICATION

possessing a firearm under R.C. 2923.13 and/or federal law. For the reasons set forth below, this Court should grant him such relief pursuant to R.C. 2923.14. BASIS FOR DISABILITY Pursuant to R.C. 2923.13. Defendant is currently prohibited from possessing a firearm based upon the following convictions (list case number, date of conviction, offenses of conviction, sentence, and date of completion of sentence for each case

State of Michigan , Wayne County
Case# [redacted]C
12/1[redacted]Robbery - Armed
[redacted] prison[redacted] 6/93
Two yr of parole 6/93 - 6/95

ARGUMENT IN SUPPORT OF RELIEF

BECAUSE DEFENDANT SATISFIES ALL STATUTORY CRITERIA HIS SECOND AMENDMENT RIGHT TO POSSESS A FIREARM SHOULD BE RESTORED

Based upon Petitioner's prior conviction(s) he is prohibited from possessing a

THE PACKET

APPLICATION

firearm. R.C. 2923.14 provides statutory authority to relieve an individual of the disability to possess a firearm. Defendant has completed his sentence, and since that time Defendant has demonstrated that he is a responsible, law-abiding individual who can safely possess a firearm and is deserving of having his Second Amendment rights restored.

Defendant satisfies all statutory criteria pursuant to R.C. 2923.14 for relief from firearms disability. Since Defendant's completion of his sentence Defendant has led a law-abiding life. In particular,

[redacted] ______________________

____

____

No reason exists to believe that Defendant will not continue to be a responsible, law-abiding individual. Other than the conviction(s) listed above herein Defendant's not prohibited from acquiring, possessing, or using firearms.

THE PACKET

APPLICATION

CONCLUSION

Wherefore, based upon the foregoing, the defendant requests that this Honorable Court issue an order pursuant to R.C. 2923.14 relieving Defendant's disability to possess a firearm. Respectfully Submitted,

Name

Respectfully submitted, /s/

___ Defendant, pro se

CERTIFICATE OF SERVICE

A copy of the attached Defendant's Application Pursuant to R.C. 2923.14 Seeking Relief From Firearms Disability was delivered to Fairfield County Prosecutor, or a member of his staff, on this ___ day of _____, 20__, at 239 West Main St. suite 101, Lancaster, Ohio 43130.

THE PACKET

APPLICATION

CONCLUSION

It can feel overwhelming trying to collect all the necessary information. I'd suggest just form a checklist of all the information you received in this chapter and knock it down slowly, it took me about two weeks, making calls, getting my deposition, remembering details of my case, printing out a generic application and filling in the blanks, it's very doable.

5

CHAPTER

FILING YOUR PETITION

FILING YOUR PETITION

You will need to make sure that you make four copies of your complete packet. A copy for the clerks office, Judge, Prosecutors office, and you need to keep a copy for your own records. You will then go to your local Common Please Clerk of Court - Civil Division (this is a civil petition) Present your packet to the clerk and tell them you are filing for your Relief from weapons disability. Do not be alarmed if the clerk is not familiar with the petition, simply refer them to the ORC code and ask to speak with someone that is more knowledgeable. There will be a filing fee involved, the cost will depend on your county. I paid around $180. Once the petition is filed , the only thing left to do is wait for your court date.

CHAPTER 6

PROSECUTOR RECOMMENDATION

PROSCECUTOR RECOMMENDATION

After you file your gun rights restoration petition under Ohio Revised Code 2923.14 or your state code, the prosecutor plays a crucial role in the court's decision-making process. Once the petition is submitted, the court notifies the county prosecutor —usually the same one who originally prosecuted your felony or the one in the county where you currently reside. The prosecutor is given the opportunity to review your petition and investigate your criminal background, current behavior, and community reputation. They may also examine your efforts toward rehabilitation, any recent arrests or legal issues, and whether you pose any ongoing threat to public safety.

Based on this review, the prosecutor provides a formal recommendation to the judge, either supporting or opposing the restoration of your firearm rights. This recommendation is highly influential but judge can still rule in your favor even if the prosecutor objects. However, a favorable recommendation often strengthens your case. The prosecutor may also request a hearing to present their stance in court, and in some counties, they're required to be present at the hearing. Like in my case, the Prosecutor was present and recommended NO! we went back an fourth like a tennis match. I would explain why I should, the prosecutor would explain why I shouldn't. Shoot your shot hard, study the code of what applies to you and know it inside and out, I had a comeback for everything.

*See My DENIAL LETTER NEXT PAGE

PROSCECUTOR RECOMMENDATION

FILED

2023 OCT 30 AM 9:39

BRANDEN C. MEYER
CLERK OF COURTS
FAIRFIELD CO. OHIO

IN THE COURT OF COMMON PLEAS
FAIRFIELD COUNTY OHIO
GENERAL DIVISION

State of Ohio,	Case No.
Plaintiff,	Judge
v.	Memorandum Contra to Defendant's Application for Relief
Defendant.	

Now comes the state of Ohio, by and through the undersigned assistant prosecutor, and requests this Court deny the Defendant, ' (hereinafter) requested application for relief from disability.

Respectfully submitted,

/s/Christopher A. Reamer
Christopher A. Reamer, 0078726
Assistant Prosecuting Attorney

Memorandum in Support

This matter comes before the Court upon application for relief from disability to possess a firearm, arguing that he satisfies all statutory criteria pursuant to R.C. 2923.14. argues that since the completion of his sentence he has led a law-abiding life and his Second Amendment right to possess a firearm should be restored.

Facts

In 1991, in case 91-003758-02-FC, was found guilty of armed robbery in Michigan and served a 14-month prison sentence. Pursuant to his felony conviction has since been precluded from possessing a firearm under R.C. 2923.13 and 18 U.S.C. 921 et seq.

1

PROSCECUTOR RECOMMENDATION

[redacted] has no further convictions on his record since the 1991-armed robbery conviction and now, under R.C. 2923.14, submits an application for relief from his disability so that he can possess a firearm.

Argument

R.C. 2923.13 prohibits persons convicted of any felony offense of violence from having a firearm unless they are relieved from disability. [redacted] was convicted of a felony offense of violence, as defined under R.C. 2901.01(A)(9), and the committed offense seems to still be on his record. To qualify for relief, [redacted] would need to be found in compliance with R.C. 2923.14.

I. Ohio Law

To be considered for relief from disability, [redacted] would need to meet the requirements set forth in R.C. 2923.14(D). Under R.C. 2923.14(D) a court *may* grant relief if:

> (1)(a): If the disability is based upon an indictment, a conviction, or an adjudication, the applicant has been fully discharged from imprisonment, community control, post-release control, and parole, or, if the applicant is under the indictment, has been released on bail or recognizance.
>
> (2): The applicant has led a law-abiding life since discharge or release and appears likely to continue to do so.
>
> FED LAW ✕ (3): The applicant is not otherwise prohibited by law from acquiring, having, or using firearms.

[redacted] states in his application that he satisfies the requirements set forth by R.C. 2923.14(D)(1)(a) and (D)(2). [redacted] served a 14-month prison term following his 12/16/1991

2

PROSCECUTOR RECOMMENDATION

conviction and satisfied his parole obligations by 6/1/1995. As such, [redacted] has been fully discharged pursuant to R.C. 2923.14(D)(1)(a). [redacted] has not had further convictions following the 1991 felony. He has since obtained further education and is gainfully employed. From all accounts, he has since led a law-abiding life in accordance with 2923.14(D)(2). These matters are not in dispute. However, [redacted] does not directly address and does not meet the requirements set forth in 2923.14(D)(3). Since the requirements for this section of the code are that the person meets all, not just some of the requirements, [redacted] should not be granted relief.

R.C. 2923.14(D)(3) prohibits an applicant from being granted relief if they are otherwise prohibited from relief by law. [redacted] states that other than his 1991 felony conviction he would not be otherwise prohibited from acquiring or possessing a firearm. This may be true but is not the issue at hand. Federal law prohibits [redacted] from acquiring and possessing a firearm because of his felony conviction and as a result, [redacted] does not meet the third required element of 2923.14(D) for relief from disability.

II. Federal Law

The federal Gun Control Act 18 U.S.C. 922(g)(1) states that it is unlawful for a person "who has been convicted in any court of, a crime punishable by imprisonment for a term exceeding one year . . . [to] possess . . . any firearm . . . which has been shipped or transported in interstate or foreign commerce. [redacted] was convicted and served a [redacted] prison term. The State courts must comply with this requirement under the Supremacy Clause and as such, [redacted] application for relief from disability should not be granted.

18 U.S.C. 925(c) allows persons to apply for relief to the Attorney General regarding "disabilities imposed by Federal laws with the respect to the acquisition [or] possession of

3

PROSCECUTOR RECOMMENDATION

firearms." Even then, the granting of relief is not mandatory and emphasizes public safety and interest. As it stands [redacted] is precluded under federal law from acquiring or possessing a firearm and as such, would not be eligible for relief by this Court.

Conclusion

Got it anyway my boy!

For the foregoing reasons, the State of Ohio requests that this Court deny the Defendant [redacted] application for relief from disability. Should the Court consider that additional legal briefing is necessary on a particular point of law relevant to the Court's determination, the State would request the Court invite the parties to further brief or supplement the record prior to issuing a ruling.

Respectfully submitted.

/s/Christopher A. Reamer
Respectfully submitted,
Christopher A. Reamer (0078726)
Assistant Prosecutor

Certificate of Service

The undersigned hereby certifies that a true and accurate copy of this memorandum contra was served upon [redacted] by electronic delivery on October 30, 2023.

/s/Christopher A. Reamer
Christopher A. Reamer (0078726)
Assistant Prosecutor

4

JUDGE GRANTS

IN THE COURT OF COMMON PLEAS
FAIRFIELD COUNTY, OHIO

ORIGINAL

FILED 2023 NOV -1 PM 12:56
BRANDEN C. MEYER
CLERK OF COURTS
FAIRFIELD CO. OHIO

IN RE: APPLICATION FOR RELIEF FROM WEAPONS DISABILITY FOR:

CASE NO.

JUDGE DAVID A. TRIMMER

ENTRY GRANTING RELIEF FROM WEAPONS DISABILITY

This matter came before this Court on November 1, 2023, upon the Application for Relief from Disability filed August 11, 2023, by Defendant *pro se*. The application was submitted pursuant to O.R.C. Section 2923.14.

Mr. appeared, *pro se* and the State of Ohio was represented by Assistant Prosecuting Attorney Sarah Hill.

After hearing testimony and considering the evidence provided, this Court finds that the Applicant has completed his sentence imposed by the State of Michigan, Wayne County Case No. 91-003758-02-FC. Applicant completed an and two years of parole. Evidence and testimony support that Applicant has led a law-abiding life since his completion of his sentence.

It appearing to this Court that the Applicant will likely continue to lead a law-abiding life hereby **GRANTS** Mr. Application for Relief from Weapons Disability pursuant to O.R.C. Section 2923.14.

IT IS SO ORDERED.

JUDGE DAVID A. TRIMMER

7

CHAPTER

Things you may ENCOUNTER

THINGS YOU MAY ENCOUNTER

IN THIS CHAPTER I'LL TELL OF A FEW UNEXPECTED THINGS THAT HAPPENED TO ME AND COULD OCCUR.

1. Court date being continued, this could or could not be in your favor, normally it's because the prosecutor is still collecting information.

2. My offense occurred in Michigan but I filed in Ohio. Michigan took their sweet time responding to the prosecutor's request for information, I called Michigan to speed the process.

3. Clerk having no clue of how to file your restoration, refer them to your state code, restoration is getting more popular now so they're starting to learn the process.

4. Clerks office not sending your packet to the prosecutor, this happens a lot, I hand delivered mine.

5. Filing this criminally, this should be filed in Civil Court. This didn't happen to me ,but to someone I was helped.

CHAPTER 8

DAY IN COURT

DAY IN COURT

When my day in court arrived I felt immediately all odds stacked against me. I was the first case on the judge's docket, he looked grumpy and tired, like he wanted coffee and to get my ass out his face. I already had no recommendation from the prosecutor, and she was evil eyeing me, with all that going on the judge asked me why he should restore my gun rights. I asked him did he read my packet, he said "no", just tell me what you want me to hear (Da Fuck). I replied "the packet is more detailed and it would help my case tremendously if you would read it"! That's how you should be in there, not arrogant, but assertive, confident , and business-like. Don't leave that courtroom and go home wishing you'd mention something and you didn't, you need to have a no regrets attitude. This is not the time to be timid, believe it or not I felt a shift in the judge's attitude when I said that. The judge stated that he was impressed with my packet, and the amount of information provided. As the negotiation for my future went on I gained a little more confidence because I read the ORC 100 times and learned everything about my violent offense, even though the prosecutor had me with the federal law, eventually I won the judge over, remember ultimately its up to him.

DAY IN COURT

The whole point of telling you a little of my court day is to leave you with these take aways.

- Know the law about your specific crime,the more you know ,the more you can fight.

- A respectable appearance goes a long way, go in with a clean look my boy.

- If the prosecutor is in attack mode just stay calm ,if you've
prepared yourself you'll have an answer for whatever they throw at you.

- If you get a “NO” recommendation still go, I almost said fuck it, glad I went.

- Write down everything you want to say to the judge, rehearse it beforehand, nerves could kick in an you forget.

9
CHAPTER

FREQUENTLY ASK QUESTIONS

FREQUENTLY ASKED QUESTIONS

Q.... Do I File this in criminal court?

A....No you file this in civil court

Q.... Did you use a lawyer?

A.....No, I filed myself.

Q....How long did you wait to purchase a firearm after restoration

A....I waited 60 days, just to be safe

Q.... How long did the process take start to finish

A.....45 days

Q.... Ever get a denial on form 4473

A.....No

Q.... what about federal restoration?

A....Apply through the DOJ 18 U.S.C 925c

Q....Do I answer no for having a felony on the form 4473?

A...Correct, answer no, page (5) on the 4473 explains it.

Q....Where to file my petition?

A...In the county where you reside.

10 CHAPTER

Meet the AUTHOR

Driven by a deep passion to help others navigate the complexities of firearm rights, I wrote "From Felon to Freedom: Gun Rights Restored." This book is my first, and I hope it's the start of many more resources designed to empower and inform.

FIND ME

Email :
Blinxgobang@gmail.com

Website :
My-rightsrestored.com

Social Handle:
@BlinxgobangRightsRestored

Address
P O BOX 1514
Reynoldsburg oh,
43068

www.ingramcontent.com/pod-product-compliance
Lightning Source LLC
LaVergne TN
LVHW022034200926
848481LV00007B/2676
* 9 7 9 8 3 4 8 5 3 7 0 2 9 *

www.ingramcontent.com/pod-product-compliance
Lightning Source LLC
LaVergne TN
LVHW022034200926
848481LV00007B/2676
* 9 7 9 8 3 4 8 5 3 7 0 2 9 *